FIND *Your* TRUTH

JAYLIN GIVENS

CoolBird
Publishing House
THE AUTHORS NEST

GOODWATER, AL

FIND

Your

TRUTH

JAYLIN GIVENS

This Journal was Created Just for You...

This journal is for people who are ready for a new beginning in life. Aren't you ready to give yourself an opportunity to be more mindful of your interior experiences? Your experiences are valid because they are permitting you to manifest into action what you truly desire. There are 15 prompts in this journal. There is also space to write under the prompts. After reading each prompt take a moment to answer the questions. Just like you I have had to endure different and difficult things. Friends, my new chapter began, and I started my business. After reading this journal and answering the fifteen writing prompts, you will be able to reflect on your life and plan for accomplishments in your future. This is a basic, yet viable approach to transform and improve yourself both personal and in business.

Are you ready? Ok...Find Your Truth!

FIND YOUR TRUTH

JAYLIN GIVENS

A Fresh Start

The beginning is the most important part of the work. Prior to starting a new business or moving towards a new chapter in your life, make sure it's a fresh start.

The anger...Let It Go! *The fear*... Let It Go!
The hate...Let It Go! *The pain*... Let It Go!

Let it **ALL** Go! You do not want to block your blessings... Especially for something so simple. Sometimes, we wonder why things play out the way they do, and why things just keep happening to us. Well friends, let me provide you with a little reminder....

- Your mouth can block your blessings.
- Your negative thoughts can block your blessings.
- Your attitude can block your blessings.
- The people you interact with can block your blessings.
- You can block your blessings by trying to teach someone a lesson who did you wrong.
- You can block your blessings by remaining in your comfort zone.

I guess you can now see that the purpose of this journal is to ***stop blocking your own blessings!*** And friends, while you're at it, get out of your own way so that you can prosper!

Prompt #1 | What do I need to get off my chest?

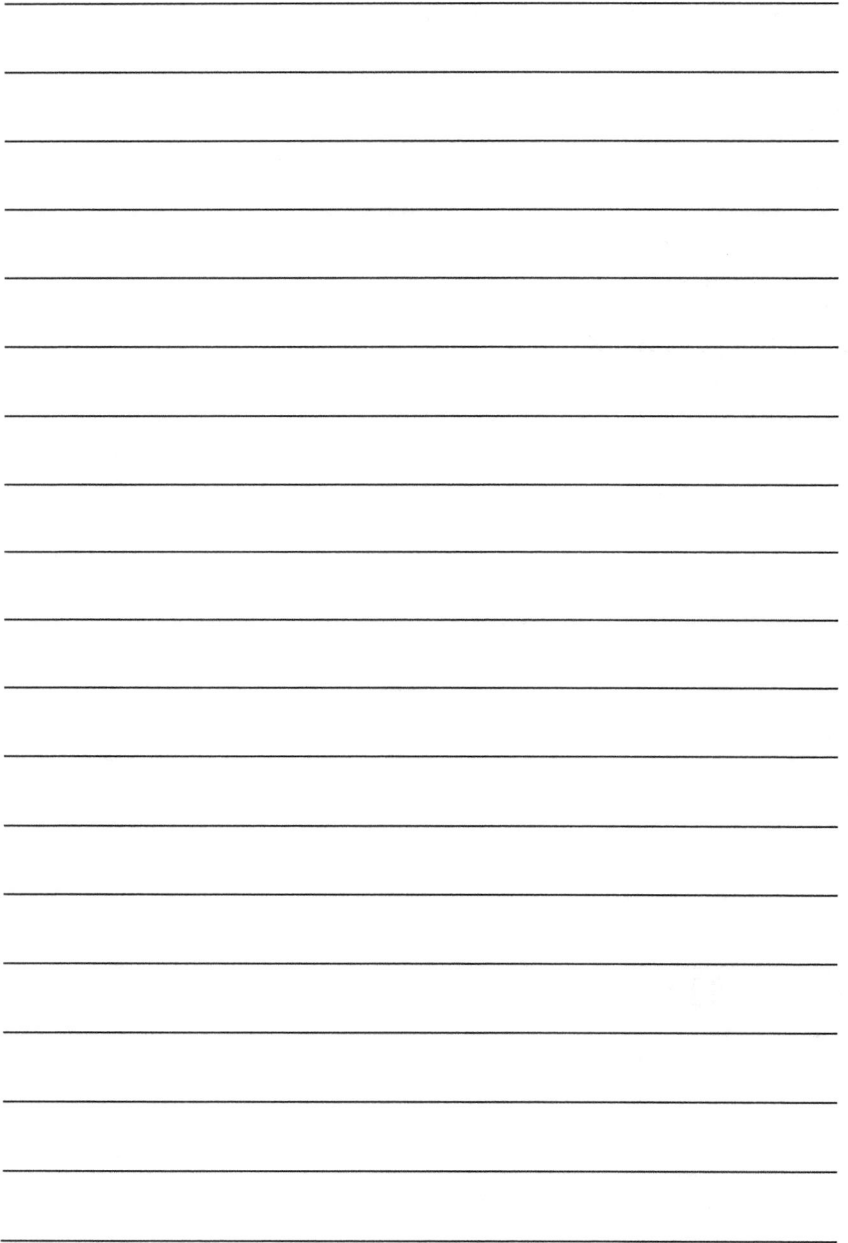

Ephesian 4: 31- 32

"Let all bitterness, and wrath, and anger, and clamor, and evil speaking be put away from you, with all malice"

Peace and Power

There will always be a time in life when we need that extra boost of energy. Most of the time we look to find peace in other people, but we must begin finding peace within ourselves. Start your day off with a smile and start your day off with a positive quote. One of my favorite quotes is "Attitude is everything, new day, new strength, new thoughts." You must train your mind to see the good in everything. The happiness in your life depends on the quality of your thoughts. Remember positivity is important to success.

Prompt #2 | What affirmations do I need to hear today and how can I uplift myself?

_____

_____

_____

_____

_____

_____

_____

_____

_____

_____

_____

_____

_____

_____

_____

_____

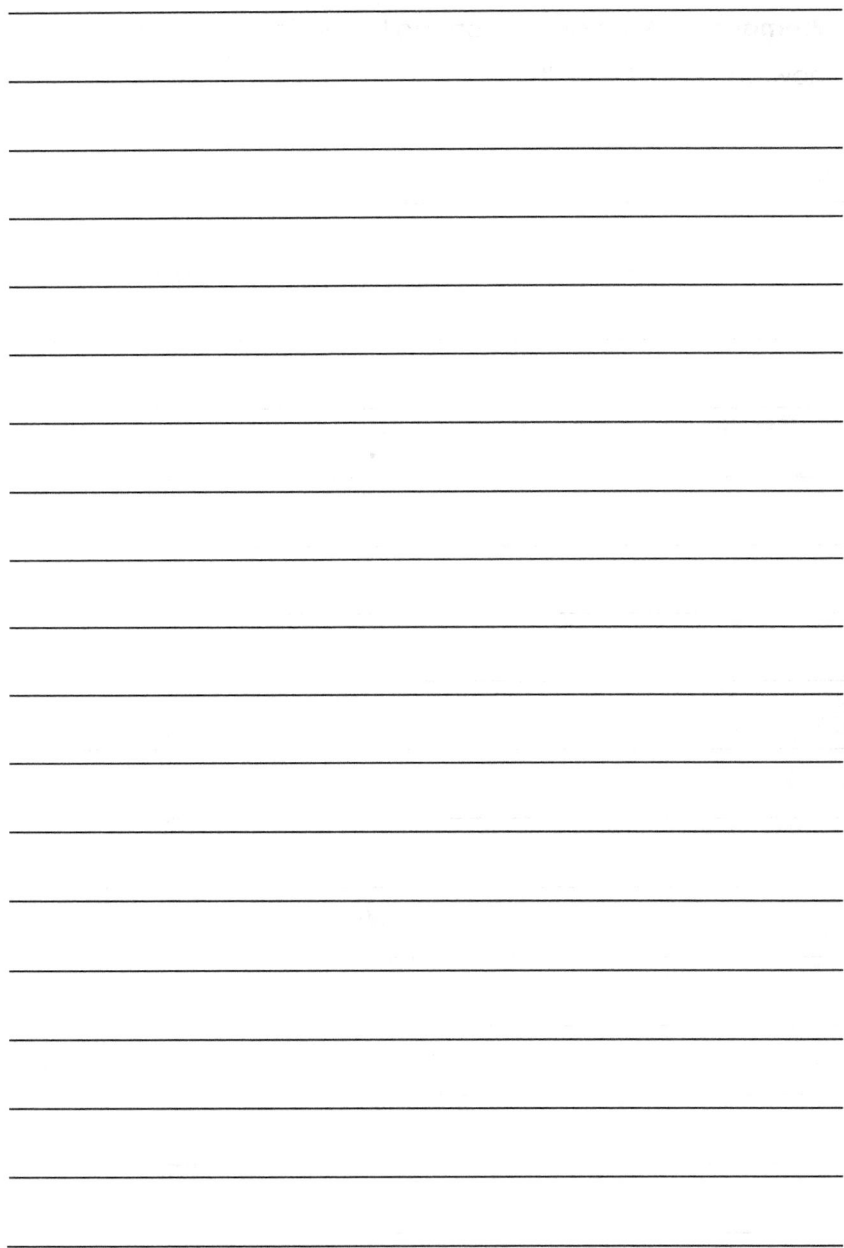

John 14:27
"Peace I leave with you; my Peace I give you. I do not give to you as the world gives. Do not Let your hearts be troubled and do not be afraid."

A Grateful Heart is A Healthier Heart

In life, there is always a reason to be grateful. It's easy to complain about all the things that are wrong, but if your actions don't change, neither will complaining change anything. If we start being thankful for everything, instead of focusing on what we don't have, life would be so much better. Sometimes, it's just a matter of how we view things. Even though you may not like where you are right now in life, be grateful that you have the ability to move forward even if it's mentally and not physically. As a matter of fact, moving forward will always start mentally. If you don't like your job just be grateful that you have one to go to everyday because some people wish they could get a job. When you wake up in the morning think of what a precious privilege it is to be alive, to breathe, to think, to enjoy, to love, and then make that day count.

Prompt #3 | At this moment, what are five things I'm grateful for?

_____

_____

_____

_____

_____

_____

_____

_____

_____

_____

_____

_____

_____

_____

_____

_____

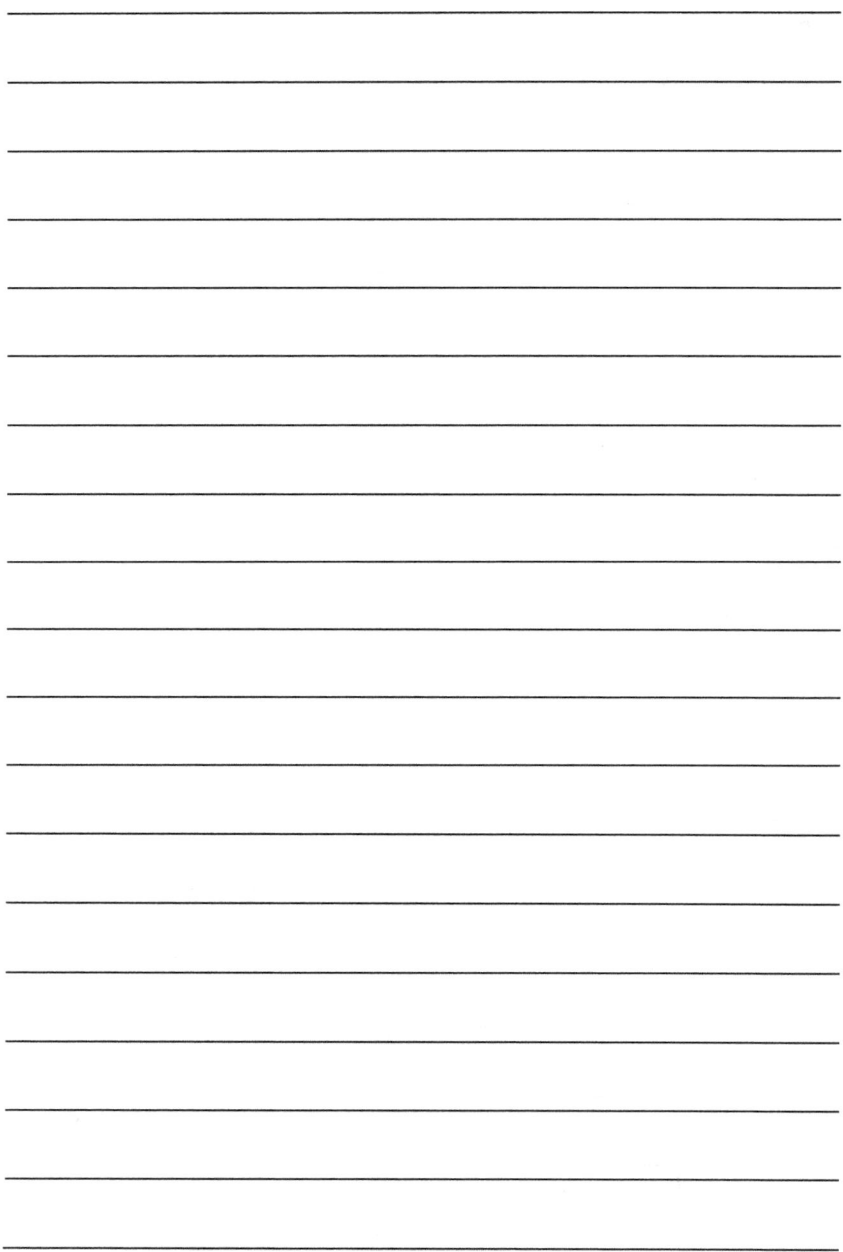

Colossians 4:2

"Devote yourself to prayer, being watchful and thankful.

Silly Me

You know as a kid, we fantasized or acted out our dream jobs. I wanted to be a police officer. I always watched the TV show "Cops" and honestly it just looked fun. Maturity is not measured by age. It is an attitude built by experience. As time went on and as I experienced different things, I eventually found a love for something else. That love was fashion and I wanted to become a fashion designer. I knew this would be something that took time. However, by the time I got to college I was still interested in making clothes, but I began loving beauty products like lashes, lip gloss, body scrubs, and other things. So, never be afraid of change and growth.

Prompt #4 | As a kid, what did I dream of becoming when I grew up?

_____

_____

_____

_____

_____

_____

_____

_____

_____

_____

_____

_____

_____

_____

_____

_____

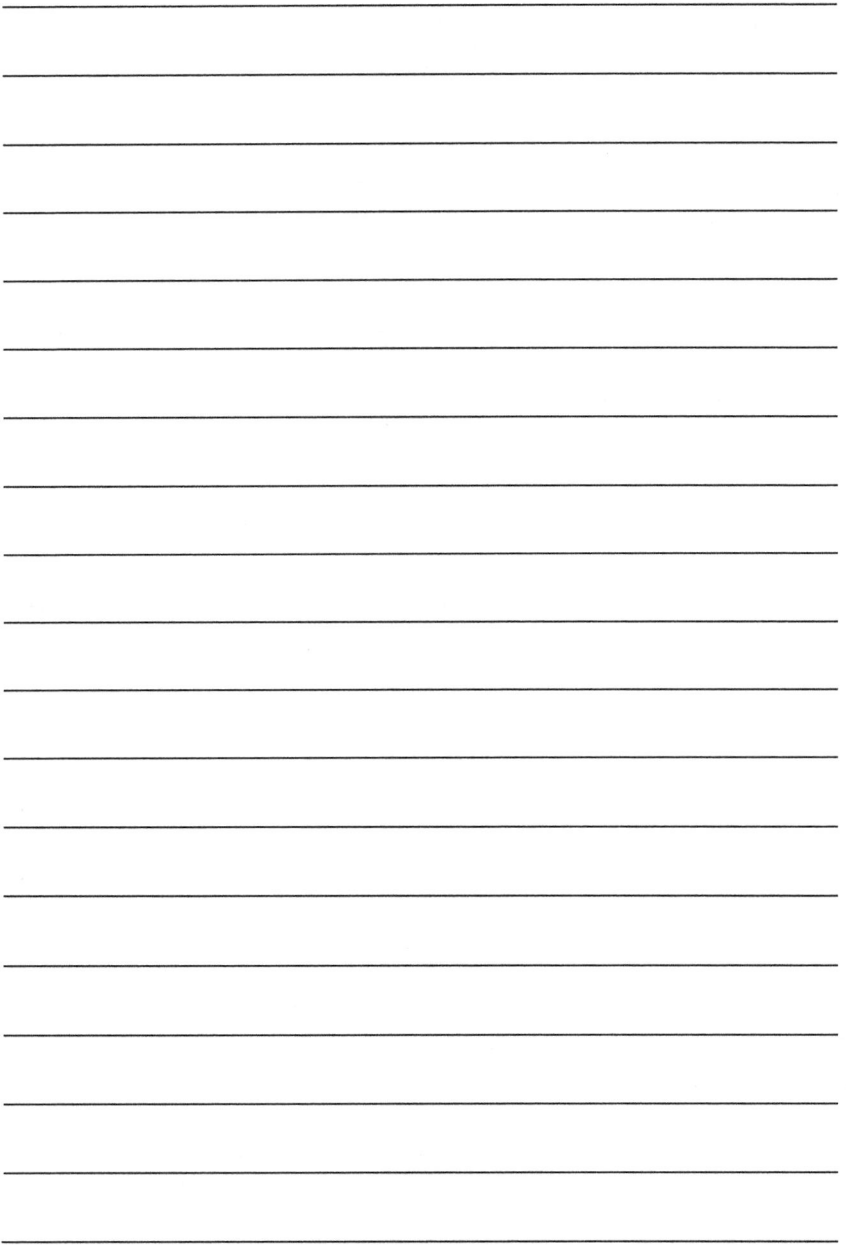

Job 12:12

"Wisdom is with aged men, with long life is understanding."

Dream Big and GO GET IT!

Your mission is what you want to create and accomplish in the future. Having a mission helps you stay focused and to make conscious decisions. Maya Angelou once quoted,

"My mission in life is not merely to survive but to thrive; and to do so with some passion, some compassion, some humor, and some style."

Successful businesses, hospitals, schools, and teams all begin with having a mission. They start by addressing how they can reach their mission. If you don't have a mission, what are you waiting on to create one? If you don't make the time to work on creating the life you want, you'll eventually be forced to spend a lot of time dealing with a life you don't want.

Pray, Believe, and Achieve!

Prompt #5 | What is my mission in life? If I don't have one, I will create one today!

_____

_____

_____

_____

_____

_____

_____

_____

_____

_____

_____

_____

_____

_____

_____

_____

Psalm 57:2
I cry out to God Most High,
to God who fulfills his purpose for me.

Knowing Your Purpose, Your Gift

When I started college, I decided to study Biology. At the time, I thought it was what GOD had instore for me. There were times when I failed and times when I passed. When I failed, I was hurt and when I passed, I was hurt. I started going with the flow of school and letting things play out however they happened, but I wasn't happy at all. I just knew that this was not something I wanted. I was lost, hurt, depressed and my family kept telling me, "*Jaylin don't quit.... I really believe this is for you.*", so I kept pushing. I still wasn't happy. There were days when I cried before class because deep down, I felt like Biology wasn't for me anymore. However, I did not stop taking Biology at the time because my mindset was focused on pleasing my family. Family is important, but you are living for you. If you are unhappy doing something, then that's not your purpose or gift. Your gift is what you are best at with the least amount of effort.

Prompt #6 | What brings me the most joy? How can I make time for it?

_____

_____

_____

_____

_____

_____

_____

_____

_____

_____

_____

_____

_____

_____

_____

_____

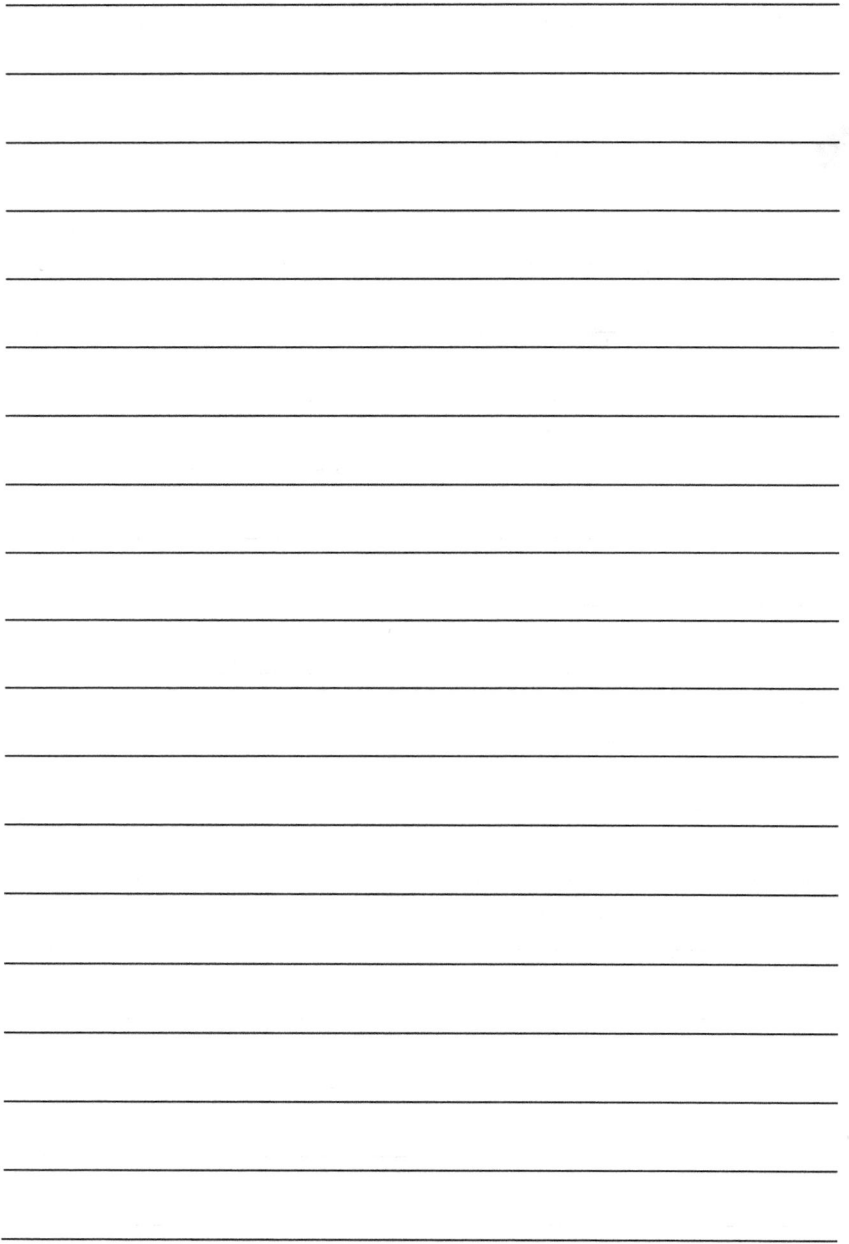

Proverbs 20:5

"The purposes of a person's heart are deep waters,
but one who has insight draws them out."

Moving Forward

If we ask for anything according to God's will, He hears us. Prayer is the key development to moving forward in life. Changing your attitude and not dwelling on the past is also a major key. I held myself back by being okay with just enough. I was okay with making a "C." I was ok with somebody else taking my place. I was okay with holding myself back. Eventually it didn't sit right with me being okay with being just an average person. I prayed for courage and strength. I started doing things I would not have seen myself doing back then. I was able to start my own business. I started trusting my opinions more regardless if someone liked it or not. I started believing in myself more. I started aiming for higher achievements in life and now look at me...I'm doing big things! Sometimes, the person who is really holding you back is YOURSELF! No more excuses!

Go live your life at a new level!

Prompt #7 | How have I been holding myself back? How can I take a step forward?

_____

_____

_____

_____

_____

_____

_____

_____

_____

_____

_____

_____

_____

_____

_____

_____

_____

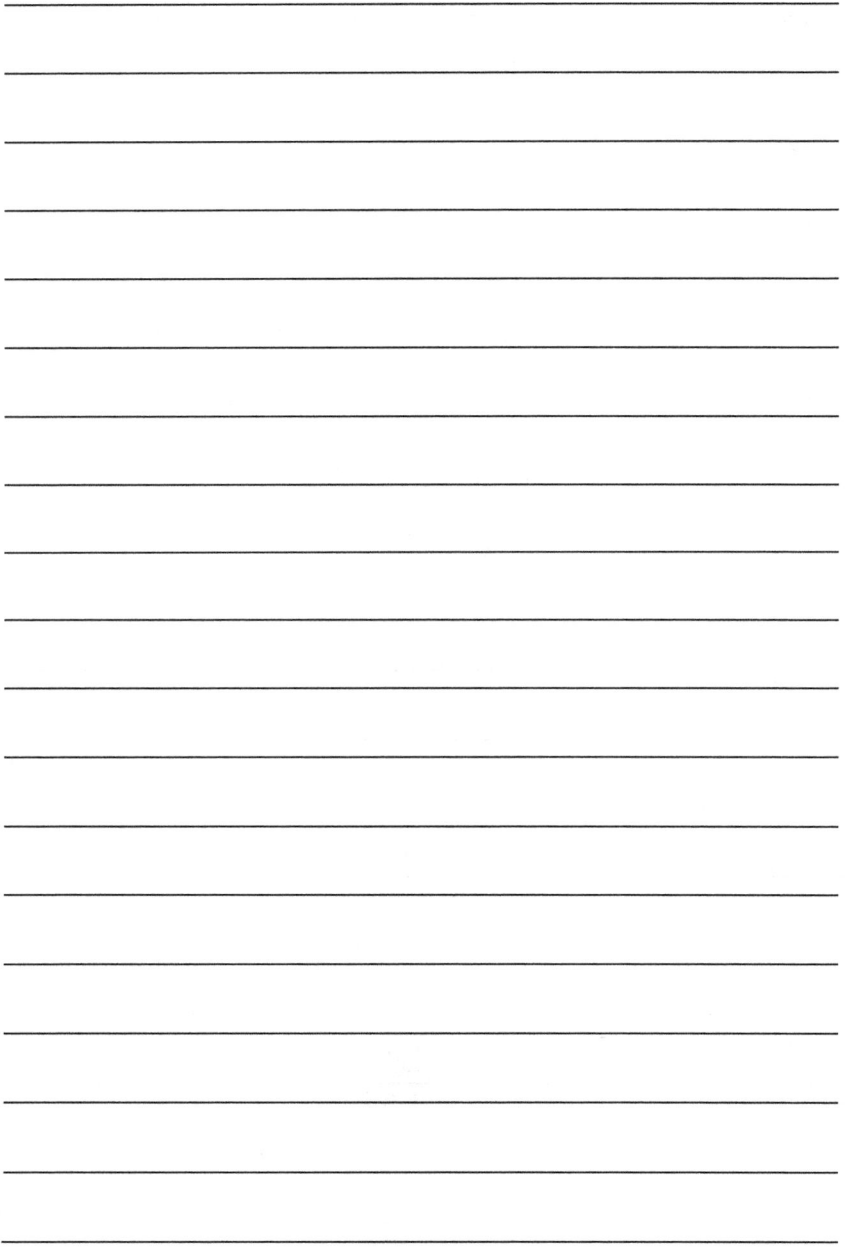

1 John 5:14

"And this is the confidence that we have in him,
that if we ask anything according to his
will he heareth us..."

A Positive Light

You must be okay with supporting yourself as well as others. I started a new chapter in my life which focused on me, myself, and I. Then, I took a step back and looked at myself and asked, *"Why be so selfish?"*. Just simply sharing knowledge can be a huge help to others. The key is to keep educating yourself so that you stay ahead of the game. The way you handle and do things can be extremely different than how someone else does it, especially when you are built for it. To support yourself, you have to take a stand for yourself. Change occurs when you decide to make it happen. Find the right path for you and then ask yourself, *"What gives me that extra boost even when I'm tired?"* Find who or what your target is and then begin to invest and build your support network. You must work for what you want; nothing will be given to you.

Prompt #8 | How can I support myself more? How can I support others too?

_____

_____

_____

_____

_____

_____

_____

_____

_____

_____

_____

_____

_____

_____

_____

_____

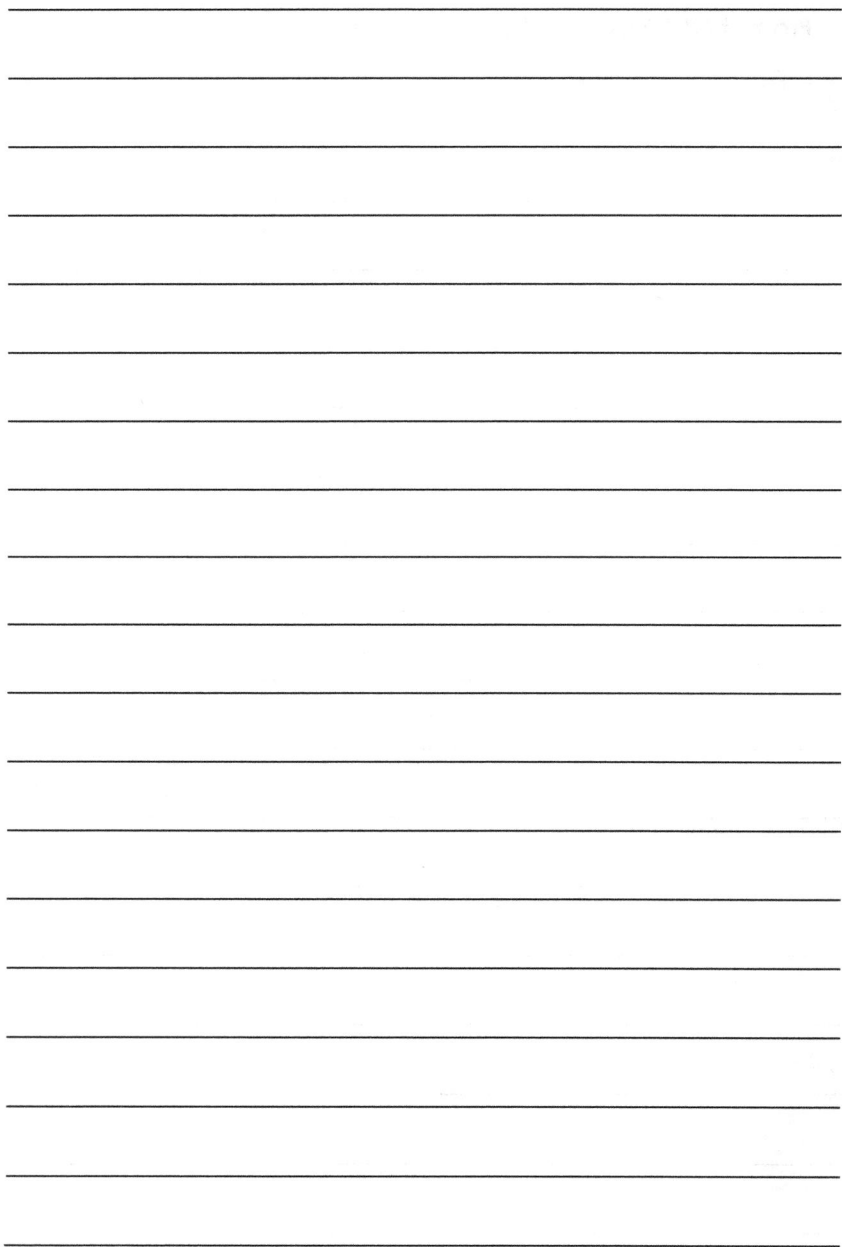

Mark 12:31

"The second is this; Love your neighbor as yourself."

Blessed Beyond Measure

I appreciate people who inspire me. All the feedback I have received since I started my new journey has made a huge impact on my life. Without the inspiration I was given, I honestly do not believe I would have been as successful as I am right now. Sure, I am not where I want to be, but I am on my way there. Next time you are touched by someone's story, blog, comment or past, let them know how it made you feel and how it was a help to you. Let them know how it allowed you to experience, discover, and understand different things, then...pay it forward! You may never know who else might need to be inspired.

Prompt #9 | Name three people who have inspired me recently and explain why.

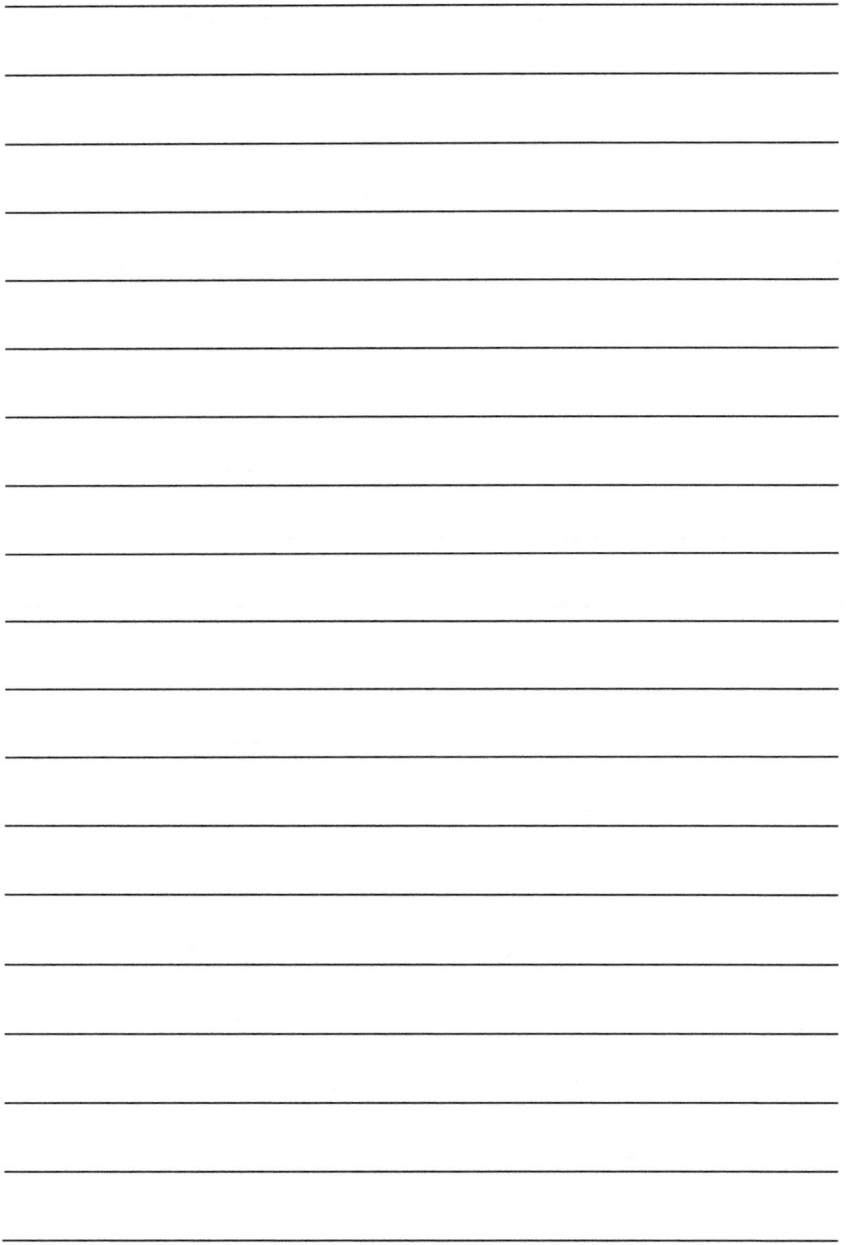

Titus 2:7

"In all things showing thyself an example of good works; in thy doctrine showing integrity and seriousness."

Speak It!

The words we think or speak can leave a huge impact on our lives. Kushan Wisdom once quoted,

"Words are free. It's how you use them that may cost you."

Speaking positivity into my life has helped me tremendously. We are the creators of our destiny and it starts with the words that we speak into our lives. Speak your dreams into existence, speak love and happiness into your life and then you'll start to notice a change in your life.

Prompt #10 | Do I speak positivity over my life and business? If not, why?

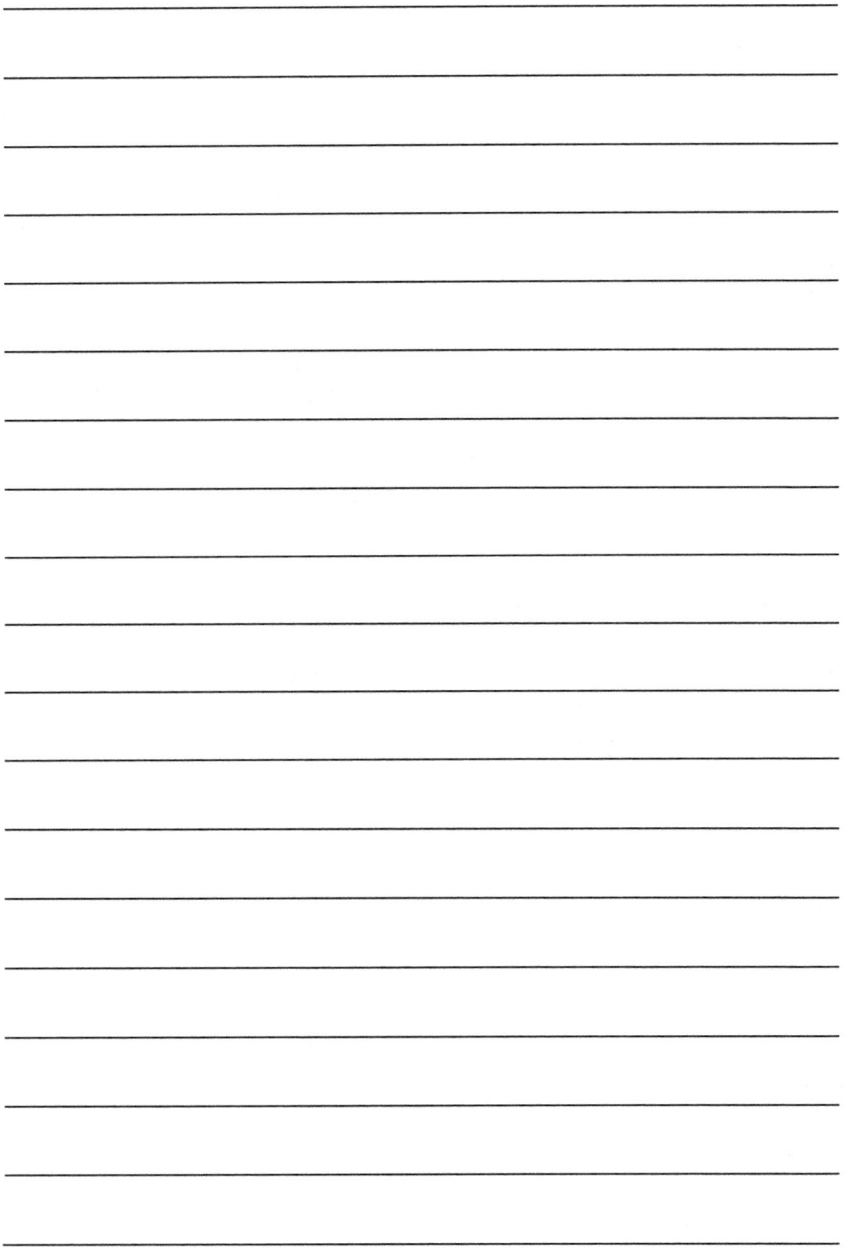

Proverbs 18:21

"Death and life are in the power of the tongue;
and they that love it shall eat the fruit there of."

No Wrath

Controlling your anger is particularly important for helping you avoid saying or doing something you may regret. Do not let the bitterness of others kill your spirit. You must learn to control your anger and not let your anger control you. I used to be upset when I first started my business. There were people that did not like my packaging...There were people who did not like my business cards...And, there were people who wanted the product, but wanted to pay later. There was so much negativity! Look, when you are a business owner, your reaction to negative vibes are especially important. Your customers are watching and so are your potential customers. When you are presented with challenges it can be tough. However, the more you practice separating yourself from your emotions, the calmer you will become. It will not be easy, but the outcome will be worth it. Stay humble and aim for the top.

Prompt #11 | How do I deal with anger?

_____

_____

_____

_____

_____

_____

_____

_____

_____

_____

_____

_____

_____

_____

_____

_____

_____

Proverbs 14:29

"He that is slow to anger is of great understanding but he that is hasty of spirit exalted folly."

Be Happy! Be Healthy!

When I first started my business, the biggest struggle that I had were friends that started selling the same product... And selling it the same way. I had people who were close to me watching and learning from the way I move. And as you can imagine, I started to get so frustrated and upset. There were times when I wanted to throw everything away, but I had a couple of real people come along to talk some sense into me. You must realize that everybody can be doing the same thing, but you can make your business stand out amongst others. A friend of mine once told me that presentation is everything. So, how you present your product or service will significantly impact your business. Hey, realize it's money out there for everyone. Do not allow negative energy and thoughts stop you especially when you are doing something you love. Nobody can take what God already has in store for you because what's for you already has your name on it regardless of who else is doing it. Listen...If their business is blowing up, it's okay. Be happy for them because you are next! It's just not your time yet.

Prompt # 12 | Do I cheer for others even if they are moving faster than me? Why or why not?

_____

_____

_____

_____

_____

_____

_____

_____

_____

_____

_____

_____

_____

_____

_____

_____

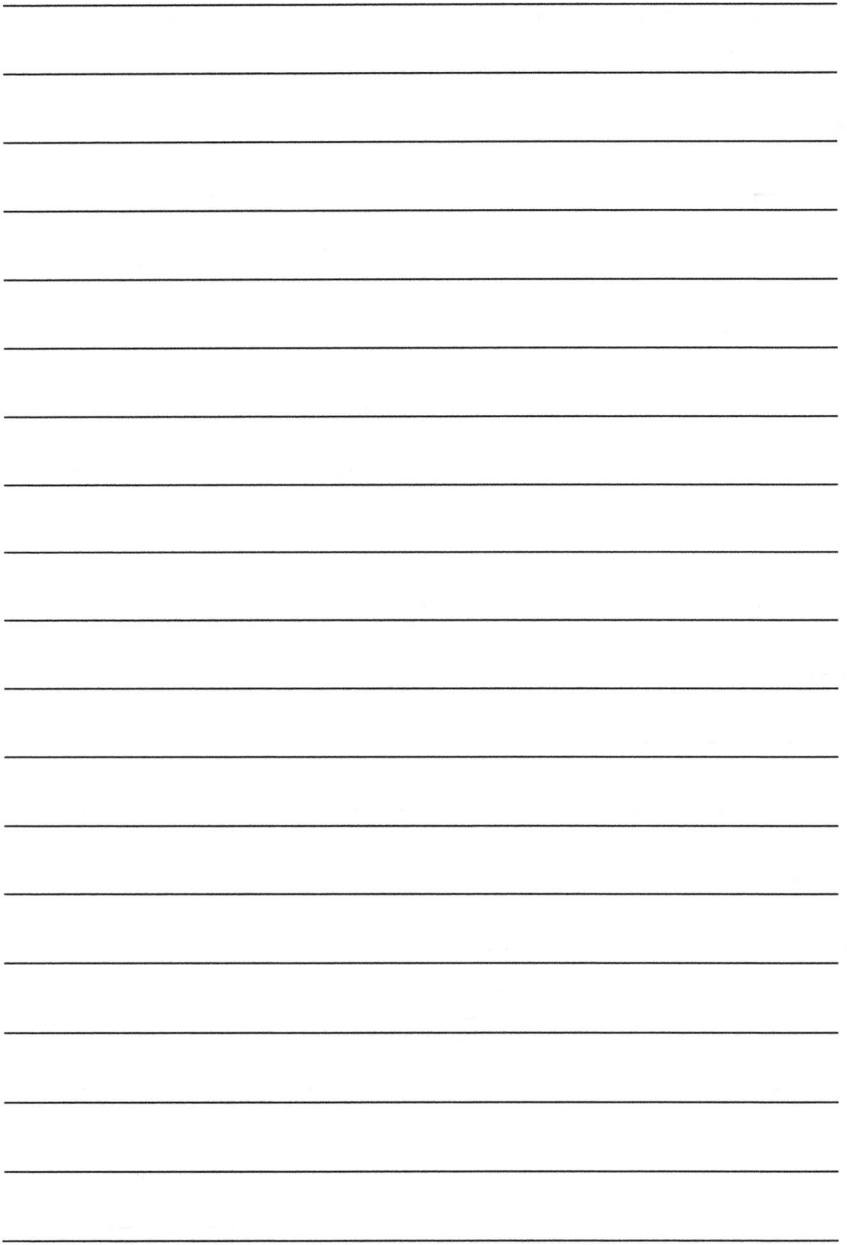

1 Thessalonians 5:11
"So cheer each other up with the hope you have.
Build each other up. In Fact, that's what
you are doing."

Take A Minute

Starting new chapters in your life will definitely take time. You will sometimes have to step back, take a break, and recharge. There's going to be days when you are just overwhelmed with everything but take a moment to pray and breathe. Everyday won't be the best but learn ways to be at peace. I always tell people do not overwork yourself. I have learned you cannot have everything and do everything at the same time. Everything comes with perfect timing. Perfect timing is God's timing and not yours. Read that again.

Grind, recharge, be patient.

Prompt #13 | How do I recharge?

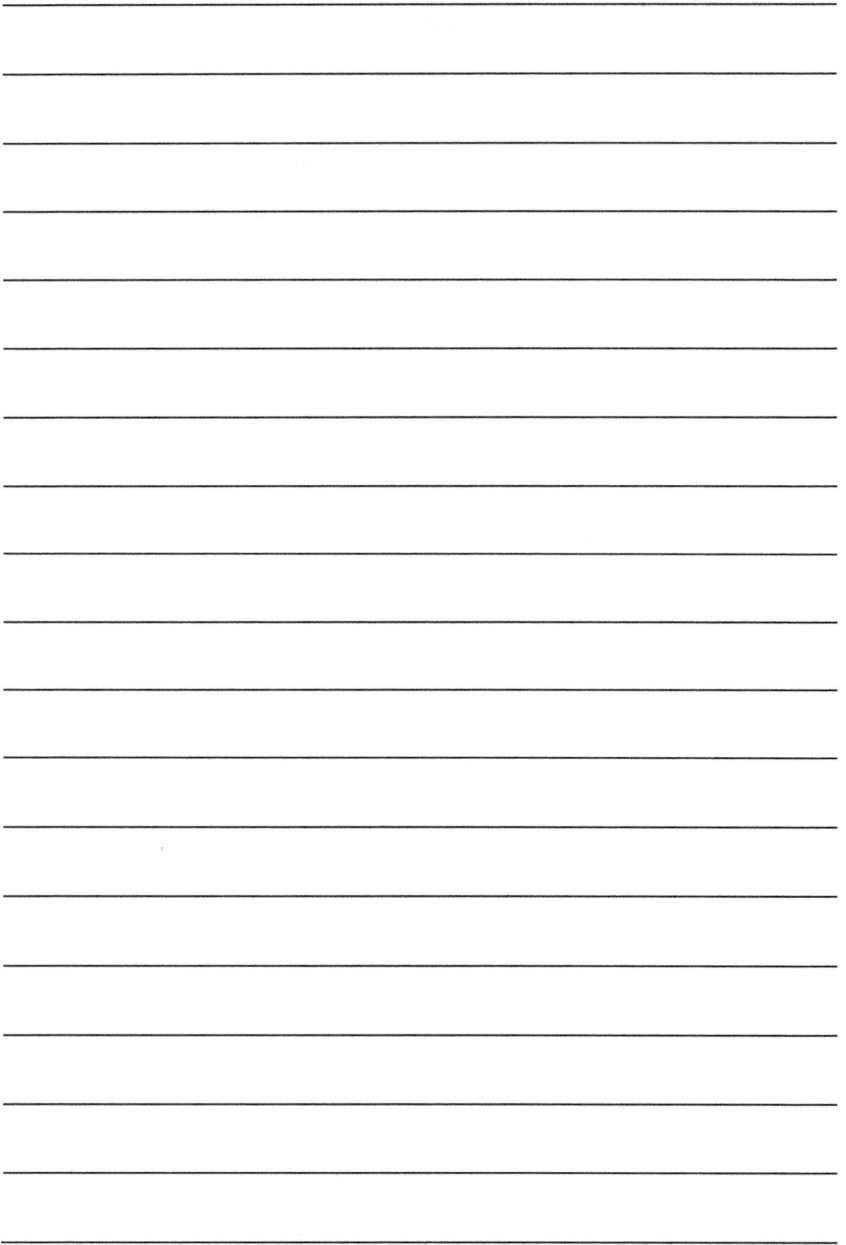

Isaiah 40: 30-31

"Even the youths shall faint and be weary and the young men shall utterly fall, but they that wait for Jehovah shall renew their strength; they shall mount up with wings as eagles. They shall run and not be weary, they shall walk, and not faint."

Thank You!

Giving back is one of my top things to do. So, I say to you, help a child in need, do giveaways, organize a food drive, just start giving! Audrey Hepburn once quoted,

"As you grow older, you will discover that you have two hands, one for helping others and the other for helping yourself."

Being able to give is a privilege, not a duty. I really love giving back and helping others. It truly brings me so much joy. If you have a business or plan to start something successful, keep the notion of giving back in mind. As you become a blessing to others, you're setting yourself up to be blessed too.

Prompt #14 | How can I give back?

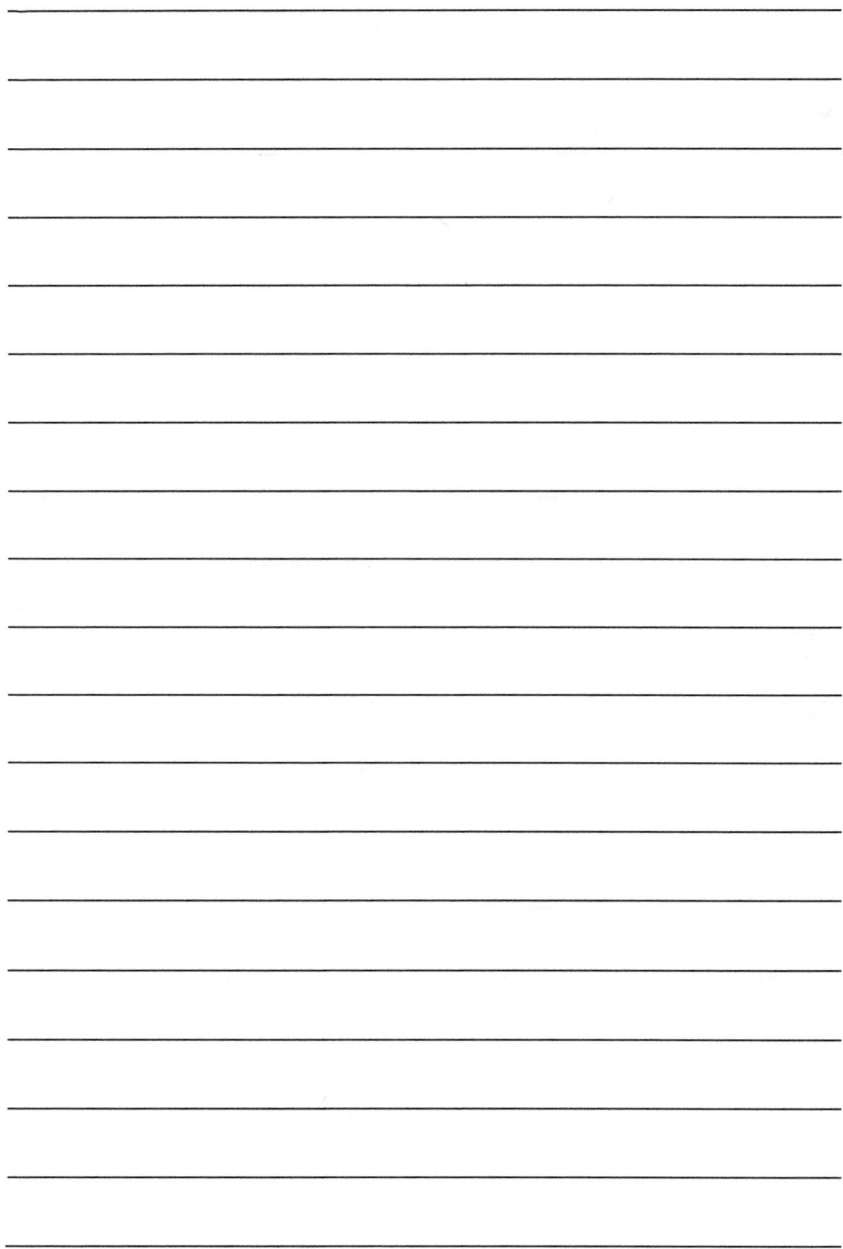

Acts 20:35

"In all things I gave you an example that so laboring ye ought to help the weak, and to remember the words of the Lord Jesus, that he himself said, it is more blessed to give than receive."

What's Next?

After finishing this journal, I hoped you received a better view of things for your life as well as your business. I created this journal because I wanted to help others with things that helped me on my new journey. I did not have a lot of advice when I started. As my business grew, I reached out to other business owners to gain insight on what to do and what not to do. I also researched and prayed daily. Learn to let go and let God because sometimes you are the hinderance of your own blessing. Remember to stay humble because if you do not, life will humble you. It's time for the new chapter in your life.

READY! SET! ACTION!

Prompt #15 | What have I learned from writing in this journal? What can I do better to improve myself? Now, turn your answer into a social media post to share with a friend.

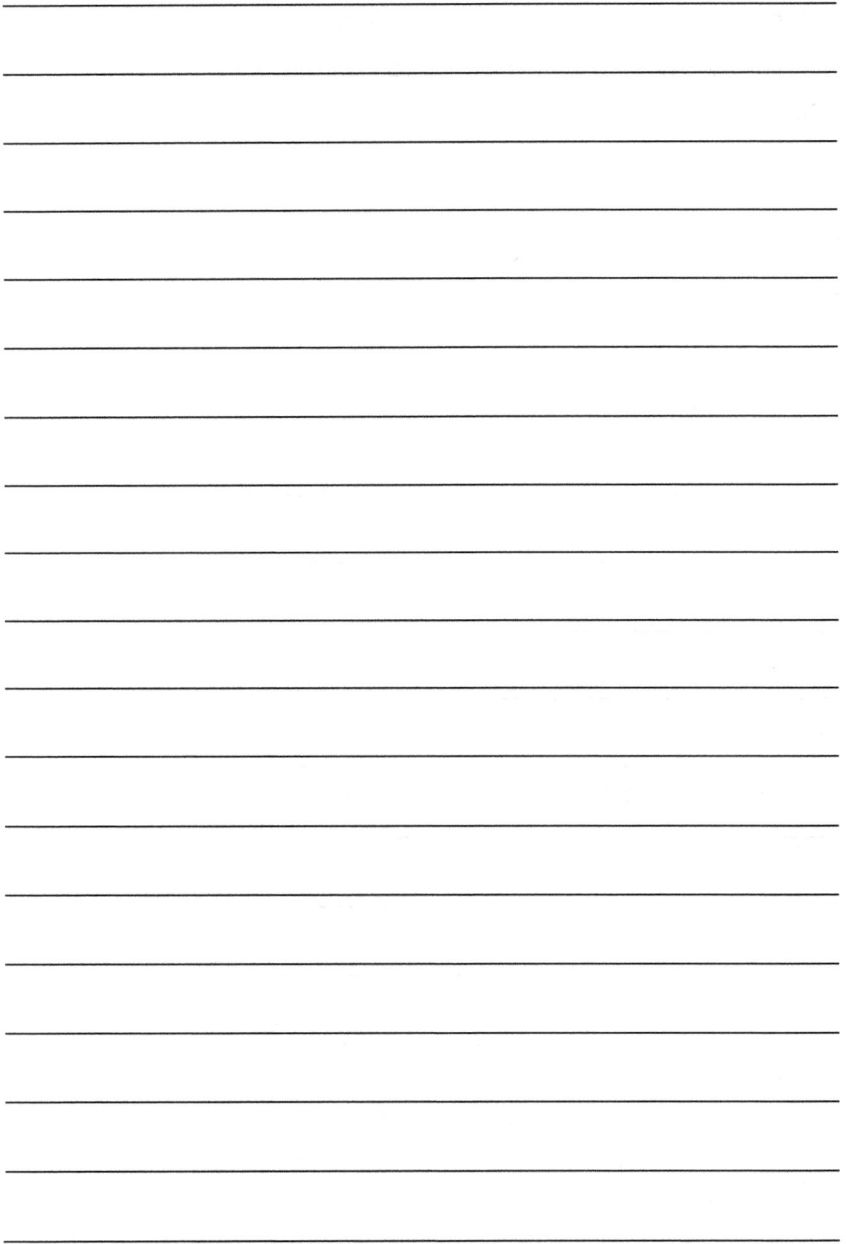

Philippians 4:13

"I can do all things in him that strengthens me..."

Fill the following pages with your thoughts, creative ideas, new networks, possible business opportunities and other amazing things! Just be creative and find your truth!

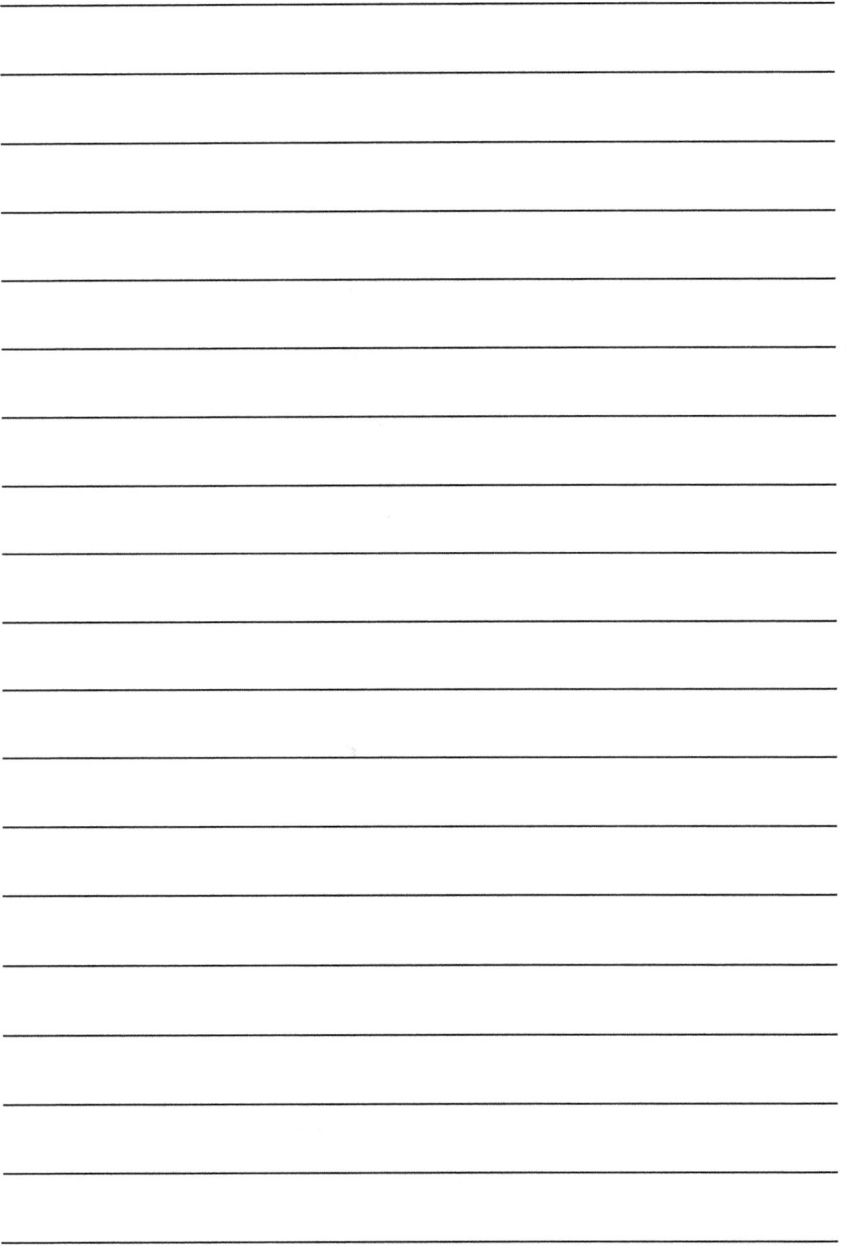

FIND YOUR TRUTH

JAYLIN GIVENS

www.ingramcontent.com/pod-product-compliance
Lightning Source LLC
Chambersburg PA
CBHW071121210326
41519CB00020B/6367